LIVERPOOL

THE COMIC STRIP HISTORY

Published by Vision Sports Publishing Limited in 2013

Vision Sports Publishing Ltd
19-23 High Street
Kingston upon Thames
Surrey
KT1 1LL
www.visionsp.co.uk

© Bob Bond

ISBN: 978-1909534-15-5

This book is 100 per cent unofficial

Art and script: Bob Bond
Cover artwork: Stephen Gulbis
Cover design: Neal Cobourne
Editor: Jim Drewett
Production Editor: John Murray

Printed in China by Hung Hing

A CIP Catalogue record for this book is available from the British Library

BOB BOND
Caricatures of many of the legendary Liverpool players drawn by this book's
illustrator, Bob Bond, can be purchased, as postcards or A3 and A4 prints.
Email **bobbond@live.co.uk** for a list of players available. Excellent as gift ideas,
for autographing, or to add to your personal memorabilia collection.

STEPHEN GULBIS
Football and art prints by Stephen Gulbis are available from **www.thefootballartist.com**

THE ONLY WAY IS UP...

IN 1959 A DARK CLOUD HUNG OVER LIVERPOOL FOOTBALL CLUB. THEY WERE IN THE SECOND DIVISION, AND HAD BEEN FOR FIVE YEARS. NEIGHBOURS EVERTON WERE IN THE FIRST...

IN THE F.A. CUP...

COME ON, LIVERPOOL— THEY'RE ONLY PART-TIMERS...

PART-TIMERS OR NOT, WORCESTER CITY WON 2-1—ONE OF THE BIGGEST SHOCKS IN CUP HISTORY...

I THINK I'LL GO HOME AND TAKE POISON...

I'VE GOT TO GO TO WORK ON MONDAY —WITH TWO EVERTON FANS !

PHIL TAYLOR, A VERY GOOD FORMER PLAYER, HAD NOT BEEN SO SUCCESSFUL AS MANAGER, AND RESIGNED...

WE NEED A BOSS WHO'LL TAKE US BACK TO THE TOP...

THEY SPEAK WELL OF SHANKLY, OVER AT HUDDERSFIELD...

AYE, HE'S OUR MAN !

WELL, LIVERPOOL... HERE I AM !

BILL SHANKLY WAS WELL SCHOOLED IN FOOTBALL CLUB MANAGEMENT, HAVING BEEN AT WORKINGTON, CARLISLE, GRIMSBY AND HUDDERSFIELD. HE WAS GIVEN THE JOB, AND ARRIVED AT ANFIELD IN DECEMBER 1959. THE REST, AS THEY SAY, IS HISTORY...

BUT IN THEIR LONG HISTORY LIVERPOOL HAD NOT YET WON THE F.A. CUP... IN 1950 THEY REACHED THE SEMI-FINAL, WHERE THEY MET EVERTON AT MAINE ROAD...

BLUES!

COME ON THE REDS!

IN FRONT OF A 73,000 CROWD, A WING-HALF CALLED BOB PAISLEY GAVE LIVERPOOL A HALF-TIME LEAD...

BOB, I COULD KISS YOU...

PICK THAT ONE OUT!

IT WAS AN EPIC MATCH, AND LIDDELL CLINCHED VICTORY FOR THE REDS WITH A FINE GOAL!

BEFORE THE FINAL AGAINST ARSENAL AT WEMBLEY, A BOMBSHELL FOR PAISLEY...

SORRY, BOB— I'M LEAVING YOU OUT. LAURIE IS FIT AGAIN...

IT WAS A HARD-FOUGHT FINAL, BUT LIDDELL WAS CLOSELY MARKED, SOMETIMES BY THREE DEFENDERS. THE ARSENAL DEFENCE WAS TYPICALLY SOLID, AND IT WAS LIVERPOOL WHO CONCEDED THE GOALS...

ARSENAL 2
LIVERPOOL 0

LOST AGAIN...

LIKE THEY SAY, THE LIVER BIRDS WILL FLY AWAY BEFORE WE EVER WIN THE CUP...

IN 1954 THE INEVITABLE HAPPENED...

LIDDELL PLAYED MANY TIMES FOR SCOTLAND, BUT WON NO MORE HONOURS WITH LIVERPOOL. HE WAS ALSO A DEDICATED YOUTH WORKER AND SUNDAY SCHOOL TEACHER, AND LATER BECAME A JUSTICE OF THE PEACE. QUITE SIMPLY, THE TEAM RELIED ON HIM TOO MUCH. THEY BECAME JOKINGLY KNOWN AS 'LIDDELLPOOL'...

LIVERPOOL LOST AT ARSENAL AND ARE RELEGATED AFTER 50 YEARS IN DIVISION ONE...

THE GREAT MATCH...

MAY 1977, AND LIVERPOOL MET BORUSSIA MOENCHENGLADBACH IN THE EUROPEAN CUP FINAL IN ROME. LIVERPOOL HAD JUST BEEN BEATEN IN THE F.A. CUP FINAL BY MANCHESTER UNITED, BY A FREAK GOAL... NOT THE BEST PREPARATION FOR A EUROPEAN FINAL...

30,000 FANS HAVE TRAVELLED HALFWAY ACROSS EUROPE—GO OUT AND DO IT FOR THEM...

WHEN YOU WALK THROUGH A STORM

IT WAS TRUE... THE TERRACES WERE SO FULL OF RED AND WHITE, IT WAS LIKE A HOME GAME! THE SINGING WAS ALL LIVERPOOL SONGS...

FROM THE KICK-OFF THE RED SHIRTS TOOK CHARGE... WHEN TERRY McDERMOTT BANGED IN A PASS FROM STEVE HEIGHWAY, IT WAS NO LESS THAN LIVERPOOL DESERVED.

IT'S THERE!

BUT DIDN'T BORUSSIA HAVE A STAR-STUDDED TEAM THEMSELVES? ALAN SIMONSEN SCORED A STUNNING EQUALISER, AND LIVERPOOL HAD IT ALL TO DO AGAIN...

WHERE DID THAT COME FROM?

ONLY A SUPERB SAVE BY RAY CLEMENCE KEPT THEM LEVEL.

NOT THIS TIME, MATE...

THEN LIVERPOOL WON A CORNER...

... AND TOMMY SMITH, OF ALL PEOPLE, ROSE LIKE A BIRD TO HEAD IN HEIGHWAY'S CROSS FOR THE MOST IMPORTANT GOAL OF HIS CAREER, IT WAS 'ROY OF THE ROVERS' STUFF...

HUH?

JOE FAGAN TOOK OVER IN 1983, AND IN HIS FIRST SEASON GUIDED LIVERPOOL TO A THIRD SUCCESSIVE LEAGUE TITLE — AND ONLY TWO TEAMS HAD EVER DONE THAT BEFORE!

WELL PLAYED, JOE!

THEY ALSO WON THE EUROPEAN CUP THAT YEAR — LITTLE WONDER HE WON THE MANAGER OF THE YEAR AWARD...

HERE'S IAN RUSH SCORING AGAINST EVERTON — ONE OF HIS 31 LEAGUE GOALS THAT SEASON.

WHY DOES HE ALWAYS PICK ON EVERTON?

FAGAN REIGNED FOR ONLY TWO YEARS, THE HEYSEL STADIUM TRAGEDY, WHEN 39 FANS DIED, MARRED WHAT SHOULD HAVE BEEN A TRIUMPHANT FAREWELL FOR JOE.

KENNY DALGLISH FOLLOWED FAGAN IN 1985 — LIVERPOOL'S FIRST-EVER PLAYER-MANAGER.
NOT ONLY DID HE LEAD THEM TO ANOTHER CHAMPIONSHIP IN HIS FIRST SEASON, BUT HIS WAS THE GOAL AT CHELSEA WHICH CLINCHED IT...

GOOD ONE, KENNY...

BY THE 1987-88 SEASON DALGLISH HAD BUILT A LIVERPOOL SIDE WHICH PLAYED A BRAND OF FREE-FLOWING, ATTRACTIVE FOOTBALL RARELY SEEN BEFORE...

THE BOSS SHOWS HOW!

PETER BEARDSLEY AND JOHN BARNES WERE INSPIRED PURCHASES, AND LIVERPOOL WERE NOT BEATEN IN THE LEAGUE UNTIL THEIR 30TH GAME — BY EVERTON, THEY FINISHED STREETS AHEAD OF THE SECOND PLACE TEAM.

DALGLISH HAD NOW VIRTUALLY FINISHED PLAYING, BUT WAS FAST BECOMING JUST AS GREAT A MANAGER.

HIS TEAM WON THE FA CUP IN 1989, BUT WERE DENIED THE DOUBLE BY A DRAMATIC LATE GOAL BY ARSENAL'S MICHAEL THOMAS AT ANFIELD...

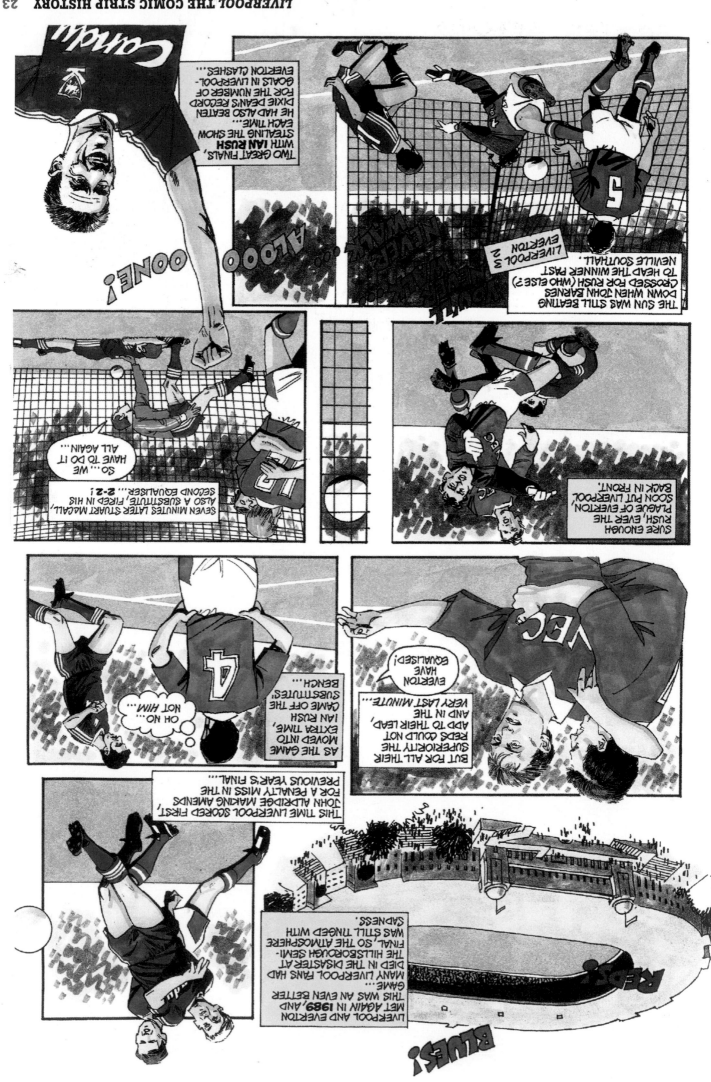

INTO THE NINETIES...

LIVERPOOL WON THE FIRST DIVISION TITLE AGAIN IN **1988** WITH **90** POINTS AND ONLY TWO DEFEATS. THEIR 5-0 DRUBBING OF NOTTINGHAM FOREST WAS GENERALLY ACCLAIMED AS THEIR GREATEST PERFORMANCE OF ALL TIME — QUITE AN ACCOLADE!

BRILLIANT!

WHAT A MOVE!

THE ONLY BLEMISH ON A MEMORABLE SEASON WAS A DEFEAT IN THE F.A. CUP FINAL BY WIMBLEDON.

JOHN ALDRIDGE HAD CONVERTED ALL ELEVEN PENALTY KICKS AWARDED TO LIVERPOOL DURING THE SEASON... BUT AT WEMBLEY SAW HIS KICK SAVED BY DAVE BEASANT! IT WAS THE *FIRST* PENALTY TO BE MISSED IN A CUP FINAL.

HE'S SAVED IT!

BUT LIVERPOOL-BORN ALDRIDGE SCORED 29 GOALS DURING THE SEASON...

IN 1989 LIVERPOOL *MIGHT* HAVE WON THE LEAGUE AGAIN... ARSENAL CAME TO ANFIELD FOR THE LAST MATCH NEEDING A 2-0 WIN TO SNATCH AWAY THE TITLE...

LIVERPOOL FANS DON'T NEED TO BE REMINDED WHAT HAPPENED NEXT...

OH... NOOO...

OUCH!

LIVERPOOL MADE NO SUCH BLUNDER IN 1990. THIS IS THE JOHN BARNES MATCH-WINNING PENALTY AGAINST QUEENS PARK RANGERS WHICH WRAPPED UP THE LEAGUE CHAMPIONSHIP — THE 18TH OF THEIR HISTORY.

THIS ONE FOR THE TITLE...

MICHAEL THOMAS HAD SCORED THE ARSENAL GOAL WHICH BROKE LIVERPOOL HEARTS IN 1989... AND LIVERPOOL SIGNED HIM IN 1991 IN AN ATTEMPT TO PERK UP THEIR MIDFIELD

STOP THAT IF YOU CAN...

IN 1992 THE VILLAIN BECAME THE HERO AS THOMAS SCORED THE GOAL WHICH SET LIVERPOOL ON THE WAY TO ANOTHER F.A. CUP FINAL TRIUMPH.

SECOND DIVISION SUNDERLAND WERE THE BEATEN TEAM. IAN RUSH ALSO SCORED — HIS *FIFTH* F.A. CUP FINAL GOAL.

DEAN SAUNDERS, A £3 MILLION BUY FROM DERBY, ALSO PLAYED IN THAT FINAL. EARLIER IN THE SEASON HE'D SCORED *FIVE* GOALS FOR THE REDS IN A EUROPEAN CUP MATCH...

NOT HIM AGAIN...

DEANO'S DAD HAD PLAYED FOR LIVERPOOL IN THE 'FIFTIES.

ANOTHER OF THE 1992 CUP FINAL TEAM WAS YOUNG STEVE McMANAMAN. HE WENT ON TO SCORE THE GOALS WHICH BEAT BOLTON IN THE 1995 COCA-COLA CUP FINAL, AND HELP BRING ONE MORE PIECE OF SILVERWARE TO THE ANFIELD TROPHY-ROOM.

ANOTHER LOCAL BOY, ROBBIE FOWLER BURST ON TO THE SCENE IN 1994 WITH ONE OF THE FASTEST-EVER HAT-TRICKS, AGAINST ARSENAL...

I GUESS HE DOESN'T LIKE US...

ARSENAL CONCEDED ANOTHER HAT-TRICK TO FOWLER IN 1995-96 AS THE YOUNG STRIKER WENT ON TO NOTCH 36 GOALS IN THE SEASON.

IN AN AGE WHEN MULTI-MILLION POUND DEALS ARE COMMONPLACE, LIVERPOOL PAID FOREST £8.5 MILLION FOR STAN COLLYMORE IN 1995. THE CLUB'S RECORD SIGNING STAYED TWO SEASONS BEFORE JOINING VILLA IN 1997.

WELCOME TO A GREAT CLUB, STAN.

CZECH STAR PATRIK BERGER SET ANFIELD ALIGHT WITH SOME BRILLIANT GOALS FOLLOWING HIS £3.5 MILLION MOVE DURING THE SUMMER OF 1996.

WE LIKE GOING TO CARDIFF!

MANCHESTER UNITED AND ARSENAL DOMINATED THE ENGLISH LEAGUE THROUGHOUT THE 'NINETIES, AS LIVERPOOL COULDN'T FIND THE CONSISTENCY NEEDED TO WIN THE NEW PREMIER DIVISION.

THE VARIOUS CUPS SEEMED TO BE THEIR ONLY HOPE OF SUCCESS, WHEN LIVERPOOL VISITED STOKE IN THE LEAGUE CUP IN NOVEMBER 2000, THEY SCRAPED THROUGH'...

THAT'S ROBBIE'S HAT-TRICK!

8-0!

IN THE SEMI-FINAL LIVERPOOL LOST THEIR FIRST LEG AT PALACE...

BUT A STUNNING DISPLAY AT ANFIELD SAW THEM THROUGH IN STYLE.

CARDIFF HERE WE COME!

BIRMINGHAM CITY FROM DIVISION ONE WERE THEIR OPPONENTS IN THE FINAL AT THE MILLENNIUM STADIUM. SECOND BEST THROUGHOUT, BRUM NEVERTHELESS EQUALISED FROM A LAST MINUTE PENALTY.

NO FURTHER GOALS FOLLOWED IN EXTRA-TIME, AND THE OUTCOME HAD TO BE DECIDED ON PENALTIES.

'KEEPER SANDER WESTERVELD WAS THE HERO, SAVING ANDREW JOHNSON'S KICK, AND THE CUP WAS LIVERPOOL'S...

WE'VE WON THE CUP!

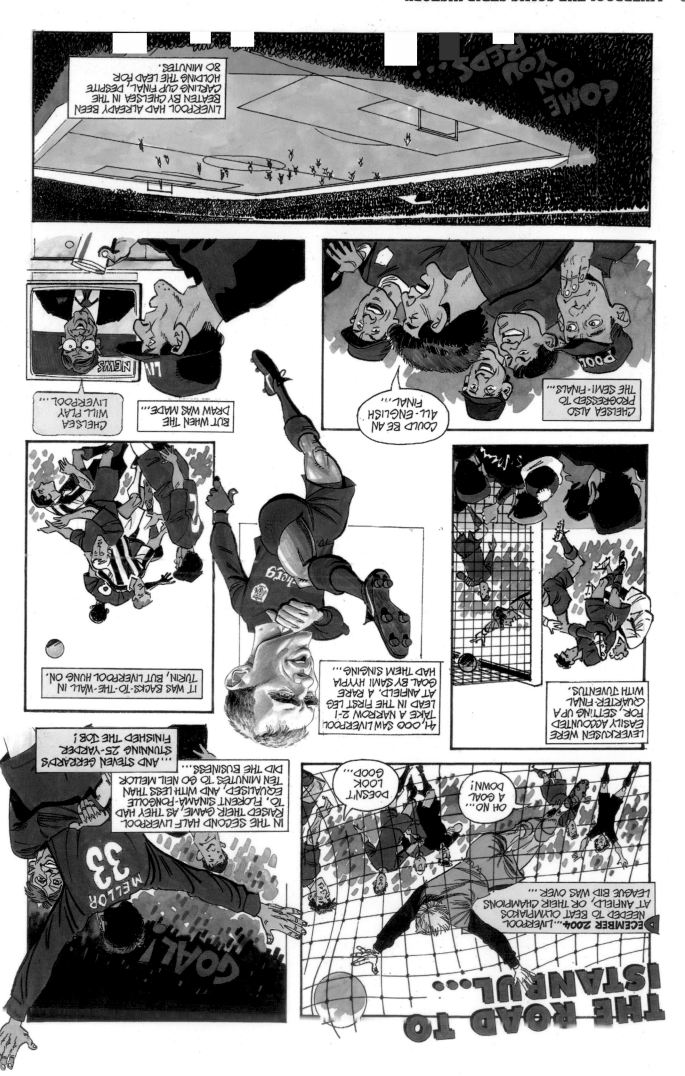

RAFA BENITEZ WAS IN HIS EVENTFUL FIRST SEASON AS LIVERPOOL'S MANAGER...

COME ON, MEN... LET'S MATCH THEM IN EVERY MOVE TONIGHT...

CHELSEA WERE MULTI-MILLION-POUND OPPOSITION, BUILT BY JOSE MOURINHO, THEY HAD NO APPARENT WEAKNESS, AND WERE ALREADY CERTAIN TO WIN THE PREMIER LEAGUE TITLE.

CHEL-SEA!

BUT LIVERPOOL WALKED OFF STAMFORD BRIDGE WITH A 0-0 DRAW...

42,000 PACKED ANFIELD FOR THE MUCH ANTICIPATED SECOND LEG...

...AND DIDN'T HAVE LONG TO WAIT FOR THE DECISIVE MOMENT...

LUIS GARCIA'S FOURTH MINUTE EFFORT JUST CROSSED PETR CECH'S LINE BEFORE BEING HOOKED AWAY.

GOAL!

NO GOAL...

HE'S GIVEN IT!

CHELSEA HAD CHANCES TO EQUALISE, BUT ON ANOTHER MEMORABLE ANFIELD NIGHT LIVERPOOL REFUSED TO YIELD.

THAT'S IT!

WE'RE IN THE FINAL!

THE BEST TEAM LOST...

MR. MOURINHO HAD TO CONCEDE DEFEAT, BUT NOT GRACIOUSLY...

LIVERPOOL DIDN'T CARE!

I'VE GOT MY TICKET FOR ISTANBUL!

BUT EVANS HAD NO GREAT SUCCESS IN TERMS OF TROPHIES WON, AND IN 1998, IN AN EFFORT TO TURN THE TIDE OF LIVERPOOL'S FORTUNES, FRENCHMAN **GERARD HOULLIER** WAS BROUGHT IN TO WORK WITH HIM.

FOWLER AND OWEN SCORED GOALS A-PLENTY, BUT LEAGUE AND CUP SUCCESS WERE AS ELUSIVE FOR HOULLIER AS THEY HAD BEEN FOR HIS PREDECESSOR.

IN 2001 HOULLIER WAS RUSHED INTO HOSPITAL DURING A MATCH AGAINST LEEDS UNITED. HE, TOO, HAD HEART PROBLEMS. PHIL THOMPSON TOOK TEMPORARY CHARGE.

THE BOSS IS GOING TO BE OKAY...

THEN, IN 2000-2001, IT ALL CAME GOOD FOR LIVERPOOL AND GERARD HOULLIER...

RAFA BENITEZ TOOK THE REINS IN 2004...

OH NO!

OH DJIMI...

AFTER AN INFAMOUS F.A. CUP DEFEAT AT BURNLEY, THEN A BRAVE FIGHT AGAINST CHELSEA IN THE LEAGUE CUP FINAL, IT SEEMED ANY MAJOR SUCCESS WAS STILL OUT OF REACH...

CHAM-PIONS!

IN THE SUMMER OF 2007 LIVERPOOL SIGNED SPANISH STRIKER FERNANDO TORRES FROM ATLETICO MADRID FOR £20 MILLION, AND HE SCORED ON HIS PREMIER LEAGUE DEBUT AGAINST ASTON VILLA ...
TORRES WENT ON TO GET 24 LEAGUE GOALS—THE MOST BY ANY PLAYER IN A DEBUT SEASON—AND 33 IN ALL COMPETITIONS...

HE SCORED GOALS FROM THE MOST IMPROBABLE SITUATIONS, TORRES COLLECTED WONDERFUL HAT-TRICKS AGAINST MIDDLESBROUGH AND WEST HAM.

YOSSI BENAYOUN WAS ANOTHER NEW SIGNING, AND HE MADE HIS MARK WITH A TRIPLE AGAINST BESIKTAS IN THE CHAMPIONS LEAGUE...

IS THAT SEVEN? OR EIGHT?

LIVERPOOL DID THE 'DOUBLE' OVER EVERTON, KUYT PUT AWAY TWO PENALTY KICKS AT GOODISON, ALTHOUGH THE HOME TEAM FELT THEY SHOULD HAVE HAD ONE OF THEIR OWN...

THREE FROM GERRARD ACCOUNTED FOR BRAVE LUTON IN THE FA CUP.

THEN ...

LIVERPOOL WILL PLAY...

HAVANT AND WATERLOOVILLE!

IN A YEAR OF FA CUP SURPRISES IT WAS BARNSLEY, FROM THE CHAMPIONSHIP, WHO BEAT THEM AT ANFIELD...

THE NON-LEAGUERS SHOCKED THE KOP BY TAKING THE LEAD—TWICE!

5·2....

BUT ANOTHER HAT-TRICK BY BENAYOUN SAVED LIVERPOOL FROM COMPLETE EMBARRASSMENT.

I THINK I'LL GO STRAIGHT TO BED...

KUYT AGAIN!

THAT'S HIS THIRD!

TAKE THAT MANCHESTER UNITED!

A FEW WEEKS EARLIER TORRES HAD DEPARTED FOR CHELSEA, HAVING SCORED HIS LAST GOALS FOR LIVERPOOL...

THE FEE WAS £50 MILLION. ANDY CARROLL HAD COME IN FROM NEWCASTLE (£35 MILLION) AND LUIS SUAREZ FROM AJAX (£22 MILLION).

MARCH 2011 LIVERPOOL 3 UNITED 1 ...TO THE DELIGHT OF THEIR FANS!

IT HAD BEEN TOO LONG SINCE ANY TROPHIES HAD BEEN BROUGHT BACK TO LIVERPOOL, SO WHEN THEY MADE IT THROUGH TO THE SEMI-FINAL OF THE LEAGUE CUP IN 2012, PERHAPS THIS WAS THE TIME...

MANCHESTER CITY 0 LIVERPOOL 1

GERRARD'S PENALTY AT THE ETIHAD GAVE LIVERPOOL A PRECIOUS FIRST-LEG LEAD...

...BUT AT ANFIELD...

2-1 TO CITY!

GOAL!

YOU BEAUTY!

WE MUST BE THROUGH!

CRAIG BELLAMY, BACK WITH LIVERPOOL, FIRED IN THE GOAL WHICH SENT ONE OF HIS FORMER TEAMS PACKING...

LIVERPOOL 2 CITY 2 —3-2 ON AGGREGATE

THEIR OPPONENTS AT WEMBLEY WERE CHAMPIONSHIP SIDE CARDIFF CITY... WHO ON THE DAY PROVED A DIFFICULT NUT TO CRACK.

THE WELSHMEN SCORED FIRST AND LAST IN A 2-2 DRAW. THE FINAL HAD TO BE DECIDED BY A PENALTY SHOOT-OUT...

ANTHONY GERRARD, COUSIN OF STEVE, CRUCIALLY MISSED HIS KICK...

JOHNSON KEPT HIS COOL, AND WON THE CUP FOR LIVERPOOL — AT LAST!

...AND A TROPHY FOR KENNY DALGLISH, SO SOON AFTER HIS APPOINTMENT,

DRAGGING DOWN JOSE ENRIQUE'S WONDERFUL PASS AND FIRING IT PAST TIM KRUL...

AND HIS BRILLIANT GOAL AGAINST NEWCASTLE AT ANFIELD HAD THE FANS GOING WITH DELIGHT...

DURING 2012-13 SOME GREEN SHOOTS OF RECOVERY BEGAN TO APPEAR, ESPECIALLY AS LUIS SUÁREZ CONTINUED TO SHOW HIS IMMENSE TALENT AS A GOALSCORER...

FOR THE SECOND SEASON IN A ROW HE HIT NORWICH WITH A HAT-TRICK AT CARROW ROAD.

IN THE SUMMER OF 2012 BRENDAN RODGERS TOOK OVER AS MANAGER.

SO IT WAS BACK TO WEMBLEY FOR A THIRD TIME IN THE SPACE OF A FEW WEEKS. BUT IN THE FINAL LIVERPOOL WERE BEATEN BY CHELSEA.

DALGLISH, AFTER A SHORT REIGN, WAS DISMISSED.

...AND IN THE SEMI-FINAL ANDY CARROLL'S LATE HEADER BEAT EVERTON IN DRAMATIC FASHION...

LIVERPOOL ALSO HAD HIGH HOPES OF WINNING THE FA. CUP IN 2012, HAVING KNOCKED OUT MANCHESTER UNITED WITH A LATE GOAL...

WATCH THIS SPACE!

THE FAITHFUL FANS ARE HOPING THAT THIS IS THE TIME FOR LIVERPOOL TO MAKE A SUSTAINED CHALLENGE FOR THE PREMIER LEAGUE TITLE ONCE AGAIN...

IT WAS LIVERPOOL'S LAST GAME OF THE SEASON, AND JAMIE CARRAGHER HAD DECIDED TO END HIS WONDERFUL ANFIELD CAREER AS A PLAYER. HE'D MADE 737 APPEARANCES FOR HIS ONE AND ONLY CLUB.

PHILIPPE COUTINHO DELIGHTED THE FANS LATE IN THE SEASON WITH SOME EXQUISITE PASSING, AND ALSO SCORED A GREAT WINNER AGAINST QPR...

JORDAN HENDERSON, A TALENTED MIDFIELDER IMPROVING WITH EVERY GAME, HE HAS BEEN AT ANFIELD SINCE 2011.

STRIKER DANIEL STURRIDGE, A JANUARY SIGNING FROM CHELSEA SCORED A HAT-TRICK AT FULHAM, AND WILL SURELY GET MANY MORE GOALS FOR LIVERPOOL.

STEWART DOWNING, CAPTURED IN 2011 FROM MIDDLESBROUGH, HAD A GOOD SEASON IN 2012-13...

A 5-0 VICTORY AT NEWCASTLE SHOWED THAT LIVERPOOL CAN GET ON VERY NICELY IN THE MEANTIME.

HIS INJURY-TIME HEADER AGAINST CHELSEA WAS HIS 30TH AND LAST OF THE SEASON, SUAREZ BEGINNING A LENGTHY BAN FOR HIS WELL-PUBLICISED INDISCRETION...

IF SOUTH AFRICAN GORDON HODGSON WAS LIVERPOOL'S FIRST IMPORTANT OVERSEAS PLAYER, SEVERAL OTHERS HAVE FOLLOWED HIM FROM FOREIGN FIELDS TO ANFIELD...

BERRY NIEUWENHUYS, ALSO FROM SOUTH AFRICA, COULD OFTEN BE SEEN FLYING DOWN THE WING FOR LIVERPOOL IN THE 1930S,

ISRAEL'S AVI COHEN HEADED A LONG LIST OF IMPORTS OVER THE LAST 30 YEARS. ON HIS HOME DEBUT COHEN BEGAN BY PUTTING THE BALL INTO HIS OWN NET !

HE THEN SCORED AT THE OTHER END AS LIVERPOOL BEAT VILLA 4-1 TO CLINCH ANOTHER LEAGUE CHAMPIONSHIP.

AUSTRALIAN CRAIG JOHNSTON SCORED A VITAL GOAL IN THE 1986 FA CUP FINAL AGAINST EVERTON...

...SET UP FOR HIM BY JAN MOLBY FROM DENMARK. BOTH MADE FANTASTIC CONTRIBUTIONS TO LIVERPOOL'S MOST SUCCESSFUL YEARS...

...AS DID ZIMBABWEAN GOALKEEPER BRUCE GROBBELAAR, WHO WON 13 MAJOR HONOURS FOR THE CLUB IN 11 SEASONS...

RONNY ROSENTHAL SCORED SOME VITAL GOALS, INCLUDING A HAT-TRICK ON HIS FULL DEBUT AT CHARLTON IN 1990. HE'S BEST REMEMBERED, HOWEVER, FOR HIS MISS OF THE SEASON AGAINST ASTON VILLA !

NORWEGIAN STIG BJORNEBYE WAS A STRONG DEFENDER FOR SEVERAL SEASONS IN THE 'NINETIES, WITH OVER 180 APPEARANCES FOR LIVERPOOL.

WHEN RAY KENNEDY JOINED LIVERPOOL FROM ARSENAL, BILL SHANKLY TURNED HIM FROM AN ALL-OUT ATTACKER INTO ONE OF THE BEST MIDFIELD PLAYERS IN THE LAND. WHEN HIS PLAYING DAYS ENDED, RAY CONTINUED TO SHOW GREAT COURAGE IN FIGHTING PARKINSON'S DISEASE.

IAN RUSH WAS THE FOREMOST STRIKER. HIS SHARPNESS AND HIS EYE FOR EVERY SCORING OPPORTUNITY MADE HIM THE MAJOR FORCE BEHIND MANY OF LIVERPOOL'S TRIUMPHS THROUGHOUT THE 'EIGHTIES.

ALAN HANSEN WAS A SUPERB CENTRAL DEFENDER. HE WAS STRONG IN THE TACKLE AND USED THE BALL INTELLIGENTLY. HANSEN PLAYED OVER 600 GAMES FOR LIVERPOOL.

KENNY DALGLISH WAS BOUGHT TO REPLACE KEVIN KEEGAN, WHICH HE DID WITH GREAT SUCCESS. HE THEN BECAME THE CLUB'S FIRST PLAYER-MANAGER, AND TOOK THEM TO A LEAGUE AND CUP DOUBLE IN HIS FIRST SEASON.

PHIL NEAL MISSED ONLY ONE LEAGUE MATCH IN TEN SEASONS! HE WAS SOUND IN DEFENCE AND LOVED TO JOIN IN THE ATTACK, OVERLAPPING DOWN THE WING. PHIL WAS ALSO AN EXPERT PENALTY-TAKER.

JOHN TOSHACK'S HEADING ABILITY WAS HIS GREATEST ATTRIBUTE, ALTHOUGH HIS SHOOTING WAS ALSO DEADLY. HE HAD A WONDERFUL UNDERSTANDING WITH KEEGAN, AND THEY MADE LOTS OF GOALS FOR EACH OTHER.

A GALL GR Live PLA

A WINGER-TURNED MIDFIELDER, **IAN CALLAGHAN** BROKE THE RECORD FOR THE NUMBER OF GAMES PLAYED FOR THE CLUB WHICH HE JOINED AS A 15 YEAR-OLD IN 1957. IAN PLAYED 846 TIMES !

WHEN EVERYONE ELSE HAD STOPPED, **EMLYN HUGHES** WAS STILL RUNNING. HIS NON-STOP ENERGY AND ENTHUSIASM EARNED HIM THE NICKNAME OF 'CRAZY HORSE'. HUGHES SCORED MANY MEMORABLE GOALS.

LIKE CLEMENCE, **KEVIN KEEGAN** WAS BOUGHT FROM SCUNTHORPE. HE WAS QUICK AND CREATIVE, ALWAYS MAKING AND SCORING GOALS, AND HE WENT ON TO CAPTAIN ENGLAND.

LIVERPOOL-BORN **TERRY McDERMOTT** WAS IN THE NEWCASTLE TEAM WELL-BEATEN BY LIVERPOOL IN THE 1974 F.A. CUP FINAL. THE SAME YEAR HE CAME BACK HOME TO BECOME ONE OF ANFIELD'S MOST POPULAR PLAYERS...

BILLY LIDDELL PLAYED MOST OF HIS 492 LEAGUE MATCHES ON THE LEFT WING, BUT WAS EQUALLY AT HOME ON THE RIGHT, OR AT CENTRE FORWARD. HE'S ONE OF THE FEW PLAYERS TO SCORE OVER 200 GOALS FOR THE CLUB...

RON YEATS WAS A GIANT IN EVERY SENSE OF THE WORD. THROUGHOUT THE 'SIXTIES HIS MASSIVE PRESENCE AT CENTRE-HALF, AND AS CAPTAIN, COULD NOT BE OVERESTIMATED... 14 STONE AND WELL OVER SIX FEET TALL,

BOUGHT FROM SCUNTHORPE UNITED IN 1967, **RAY CLEMENCE** DIDN'T MAKE HIS FIRST-TEAM DEBUT UNTIL JANUARY 1970. WONDERFULLY CONSISTENT, HE THEN PLAYED 579 LEAGUE AND CUP MATCHES IN GOAL BEFORE MOVING TO SPURS IN 1981. CLEMENCE ALSO WON 61 ENGLAND CAPS.

THIS IS
LIVER POOL FOOTBALL CLUB
ANFIELD

FACTS & FIGURES

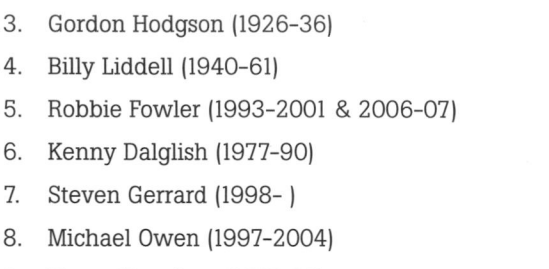

All-time top goalscorers

1.	Ian Rush (1980–87 & 1988–96)	346
2.	Roger Hunt (1959–69)	286
3.	Gordon Hodgson (1926–36)	241
4.	Billy Liddell (1940–61)	228
5.	Robbie Fowler (1993–2001 & 2006–07)	183
6.	Kenny Dalglish (1977–90)	172
7.	Steven Gerrard (1998–)	159
8.	Michael Owen (1997–2004)	158
9.	Harry Chambers (1915–28)	151
10.	Jack Parkinson (1903–14)	130

RECORDS

Record win

11–0 v Stromsgodset (H), European Cup Winners Cup first round, first leg, 17th September 1974

Record defeat

1–9 v Birmingham City (A), Division Two, 11th December 1954

HONOURS

First Division championship: 1900/01, 1905/06, 1921/22, 1922/23, 1946/47, 1963/64, 1965/66, 1972/73, 1975/76, 1976/77, 1978/79, 1979/80, 1981/82, 1982/83, 1983/84, 1985/86, 1987/88, 1989/90

Second Division championship: 1893/94, 1895/96, 1904/05, 1961/62

FA Cup: 1965, 1974, 1986, 1989, 1992, 2001, 2006

League Cup: 1981, 1982, 1983, 1984, 1995, 2001, 2003, 2012

Screen Sport Super Cup: 1986

Charity Shield/Community Shield: 1964*, 1965*, 1966, 1974, 1976, 1977*, 1980, 1982, 1986*, 1988, 1989, 1990*, 2001, 2006 (* joint winners)

European Cup/Champions League: 1977, 1978, 1981, 1984, 2005

Uefa Cup: 1973, 1976, 2001

Uefa Super Cup: 1977, 2001, 2005

All-time top appearance makers

1.	Ian Callaghan (1960–78)	857
2.	Jamie Carragher (1997–2013)	737
3.=	Ray Clemence (1967–81)	665
3.=	Emlyn Hughes (1967–79)	665
5.	Ian Rush (1980–87 & 1988–96)	660
6.	Phil Neal (1974–85)	650
7.	Tommy Smith (1963–78)	638
8.	Steven Gerrard (1998–)	630
9.	Bruce Grobbelaar (1981–94)	628
10.	Alan Hansen (1977–91)	620

Most goals in a match by one player

5 John Miller v Fleetwood Rangers (H), Lancashire
League, 3rd December 1892

5 Andy McGuigan v Stoke (H), Division One,
4th January 1902

5 John Evans v Bristol Rovers (H), Division Two,
15th September 1954

5 Ian Rush v Luton Town (H), Division One,
29th October 1983

5 Robbie Fowler v Fulham (H), League Cup,
5th October 1993

Most hat-tricks

17 Gordon Hodgson (1926-36)

16 Ian Rush (1980-86 & 1988-96)

12 Roger Hunt (1959-69)

10 Robbie Fowler (1993-2001 & 2006-07)

10 Michael Owen (1997-2004)

Most consecutive games played

1. Phil Neal (1976-83)   417
2. Ray Clemence (1972-78)   336
3. Bruce Grobbelaar (1981-86)   317
4. Chris Lawler (1965-71)   316
5. David James (1994-98)   213

PREMIERSHIP RECORDS

Most Premiership appearances

1. Jamie Carragher (1997-2013)   508
2. Steven Gerrard (1998-)   441
3. Sami Hyypia (1999-2009)   318

Most Premiership goals

1. Robbie Fowler (1993-2001 & 2006-07)   128
2. Michael Owen (1997-2004)   118
3. Steven Gerrard (1998-)   98

Milestone Premiership goals

Date	Goal	Scorer	Opponents
19/8/92	1	Mark Walters	Sheffield Utd (H)
4/1/94	100	Nigel Clough	Manchester Utd (H)
1/10/95	200	Robbie Fowler	Manchester Utd (A)
19/2/97	300	Stan Collymore	Leeds Utd (H)
24/10/98	400	Michael Owen	Nottingham Forest (H)
1/4/2000	500	Michael Owen	Coventry City (A)
8/12/01	600	Michael Owen	Middlesbrough (H)
26/4/03	700	Michael Owen	West Brom (A)
5/2/05	800	Milan Baros	Fulham (H)
1/1/07	900	Dirk Kuyt	Bolton (H)
5/10/08	1000	Fernando Torres	Manchester City (A)
29/11/09	1100	Dirk Kuyt	Everton (A)
15/10/11	1200	Steven Gerrard	Manchester Utd (H)
27/4/13	1300	Daniel Sturridge	Newcastle Utd (A)

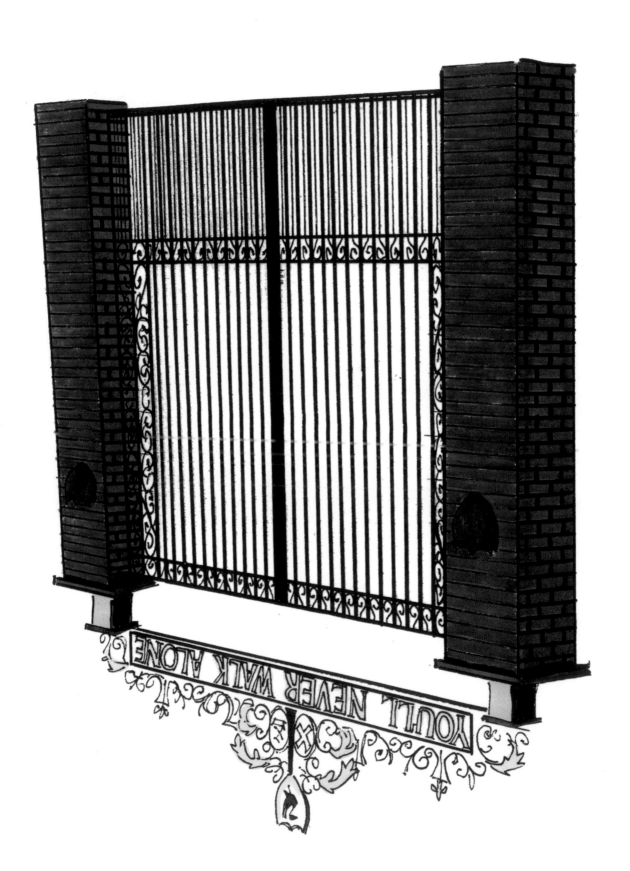